IN DEDICATION TO
ANTOINETTE TOLMAIRE BROWN

EXODUS 20:12

CONTENTS

HOW TO USE
THIS RESOURCE

1-2

INTRODUCTION

3-6

PATIENTLY
ENDURE

7-10

FORGIVE
INSTANTLY

11-14

LET GO
QUICKLY

15-18

LOVE
UNCONDITIONALLY

19-23

HOW GOD CAN
TURN MY PAIN
INTO PURPOSE

24-27

How To Use This Resource

As humans, we have absolutely nothing to offer humanity except the message of Jesus. This guide is precisely designed to direct you to Jesus and the Cross of Calvary. In the pages to come you will find nothing but scripture and prayers that have been written at the direction of the Holy Spirit.

My hope is that you will use this as a starting point in your devotional or reflection time before the Lord. It is designed to help guide you through scripture showing where and how to begin letting go.

With each step you will find the following:

Study- The Bible makes it clear that "All scripture is inspired by God". What better way to seek God than going directly to his written word for us. Take time not only to open your own Bible, but to mediate on his Word and how it is applicable to your life today. If you are in need of a Bible and do not have the means to purchase one, please email us at info@revivedcommunity.com

Prayer- The Lord desires to speak to us. Scripture says that He is a "rewarder to those who diligently seek him". Whether early in the morning, during your day or late at night make time to get away and be alone with the Lord. Find a quiet place to fully rest before the Lord and listen for what He has to say.

Reflection- The Holy Spirit desires to bring conviction to our hearts in order to draw us to Jesus. After you have read the Word and have taken time to listen, take the next step to obey. Reflect on what the Lord is saying and commit to taking action TODAY. Do not wait, our tomorrow is not promised.

You do not have to walk through hardships alone. The Lord designed us to be in unity, together, and fight our battles in prayer. **If you need prayer or desire to know more about the Lord contact us at prayer@revivedcommunity.com**

2 CORINTHIANS 12:9

Introduction

"Each time he said, "My grace is all you need. My power works best in weakness." So now I am glad to boast about my weaknesses, so that the power of Christ can work through me." 2 Corinthians 12:9

Prayer

Abba Father, thank You! Thank you that You strengthen me to patiently endure, forgive instantly, let go quickly, and love unconditionally. I count it all JOY! For the joy of You is my strength. (Nehemiah 8:10) Your power works best in my weakness and You are an ever present help in times of trouble. (Psalm 36:1) Thank You Father for **I am not alone because You are with me**. I surrender it all to you: the trauma, the depression, the addictions, the anger and fear, the bitterness and jealousy, the malice, the battles and scars. I denounce any and all ties to witchcraft and manipulation.

Cleanse my heart, purify my mind, renew a right spirit within me. (Psalm. 51:10-12) Take it all away Jesus! I am healed by YOU! By Your stripes, I am healed and set free. Who the Father sets free, is free indeed! Thank You for saving me. For freeing me from sin and evil. I resist the devil and call upon the name of Jesus which causes satan to flee. (James 4:7)

I am your temple. I am a house of prayer dedicated and loyal to You Jesus. Thank You Abba, Father. I am free and my pain now has a purpose to glorify You! **May my life glorify You Lord.** I am Yours and You are my Father.

By the blood of the Lamb that died for me... In Jesus name...Amen

JESUS, I TRUST YOU WITH:

"That's why I take pleasure in my weaknesses, and in the insults, hardships, persecutions, and troubles that I suffer for Christ. For when I am weak, then I am strong."
2 Corinthians 12:10

1 PETER 2:20

Patiently Endure

Study

"19 For God is pleased when, <u>conscious of his will</u>, **you patiently endure** unjust treatment. 20 Of course, you get no credit for being patient if you are beaten for doing wrong. But if you suffer for doing good and **endure it patiently**, God is pleased with you. 21 For God called you to do good, <u>even if it means suffering, just as Christ suffered for you</u>. He is your example, and you must follow in his steps. 22 He never sinned, nor ever deceived anyone. 23 **He did not retaliate** when he was insulted, nor threaten revenge when he suffered. He left his case in the hands of God, who always judges fairly. 24 He <u>personally carried our sins in his body</u> on the cross so that we can be dead to sin and live for what is right. By his wounds you are healed."
1 Peter 2:19-24

Prayer

Father in Heaven, may the trials of life teach me to be conscious of Your will and to endure patiently. I no longer desire to allow pain, heartache, and harsh words to turn into a rage of bitter emotions that control my life. May I understand that there is a purpose for every tear and may I see You in all the hardship that I face for Your name's sake. Give me the strength to leave every case in Your hands Father. May I never sin, deceive others, retaliate, nor threaten others in Jesus name. Father, teach me to endure patiently just as You did. Amen.

JESUS, I WILL PATIENTLY ENDURE:

"No, dear brothers and sisters, I have not achieved it, but I focus on this one thing: Forgetting the past and looking forward to what lies ahead"
Philippians 3:13

EPHESIANS 4:32

Forgive Instantly

Study

"Jesus said, "Father, forgive them, for they don't know what they are doing." And the soldiers gambled for his clothes by throwing dice." **Luke 23:34**

"Create in me a clean heart, O God. Renew a loyal spirit within me." Psalms 51:10

Prayer

Father in Heaven, after enduring the most inhumane beating and torture **You** said Father, forgive them, for they don't know what they are doing." (Luke 23:34) May You remove all pride that keeps me from forgiving those who have hurt me. I desire to forgive but sometimes I do not truly understand how or even why it feels impossible. You died so that my sins may be forgiven and I thank you for showing such grace and mercy to me. Father, **teach my heart to do the same for others**. Create a new heart in me that forgives instantly and renew a loyal spirit in me that will follow Your decrees always. May I give the same forgiveness, grace, and mercy that You did on that cross for me.

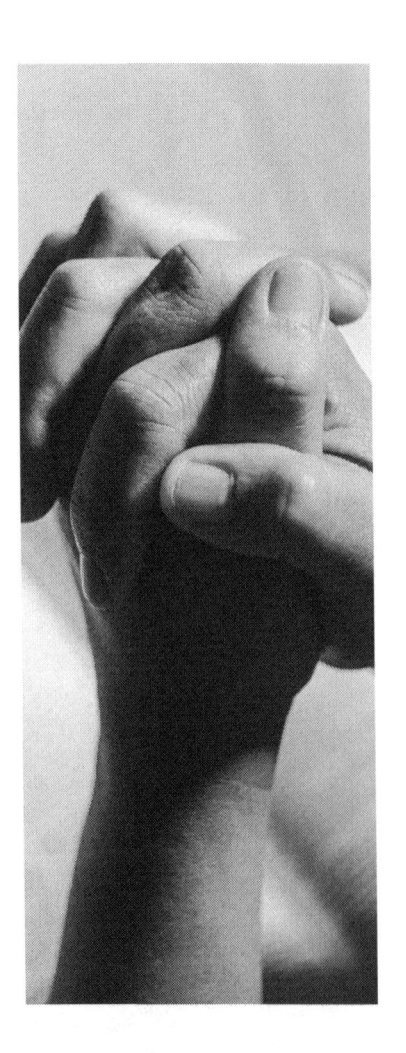

Biblically, forgiveness is **NOT** a process: It is a **CHOICE!** Jesus CHOSE to forgive those who persecuted him while it was still happening. The world would have us believe that we must remain in the process of forgiveness so that we will not feel responsible to forgive today as Christ did. Healing is a process but **the process of healing cannot begin until the CHOICE of forgiveness is made first.**

JESUS, AS YOU DID, SO I CHOOSE TO FORGIVE:

"3 We can **rejoice**, too, when we run into problems and trials, for we know that they help us **develop endurance**. 4 And endurance develops **strength of character**, and character strengthens our **confident hope** of salvation. 5 And <u>this hope will not lead to disappointment</u>. For we know how dearly God loves us, because he has given us the Holy Spirit to fill our hearts with his love."
Romans 5:3-5

MATTHEW 6:14

Let Go Quickly

Study

"13 No, dear brothers and sisters, I have not achieved it, but I focus on this one thing: **Forgetting the past and looking forward** to what lies ahead, 14 I press on to reach the end of the race and receive the heavenly prize for which God, through Christ Jesus, is calling us. 15 Let all who are spiritually mature agree on these things. If you disagree on some point, I believe God will make it plain to you. 16 But **we must hold on to the progress** we have already made." **Philippians 3:13-16**

Be Still derives from the word Rapha. Jehovah Rapha is Our God who heals. Be Still in Hebrew means to be in a weak state, to release and let go. When we release and let go of the burdens and trauma that we carry, Jehovah Rapha comes in & heals our hearts!

<u>WILL YOU LET GO OF THE PAST TODAY</u>
<u>AND NOT LOOK BACK</u> <u>LIKE LOT'S WIFE?</u>

"But Lot's wife looked back as she was following behind him, and she turned into a pillar of salt."
Genesis 19:26

Prayer

Abba Father, teach me to **let go and release** my past trauma, pain and hurt to You! You are Jehovah Rapha, Our God who heals. Heal my heart and take away all emotions tied to my past! Paul said that he focuses on this one thing: **letting go of the past and focusing on what lies ahead.**

Father I do not wish to be stuck as a pillar of salt by looking back, I desire to focus on what lies ahead- Your Glory! I wish to run this race with endurance to reach the heavenly prize that You have for me. Abba Father, make this plain to my heart and give me strength to release this all to You. Heal my hurt so that my eyes and mind will never look back. May I Be Still in Your presence!

JESUS, TODAY I LET GO OF:

"Cast all your anxiety on him because he cares for you."
1 Peter 5:7

EPHESIANS 4:32

Love Unconditionally

Study ♡

"7 Dear friends, let us continue to **love** one another, for **love** comes from God. Anyone who **loves** is a child of God and knows God. 8 But anyone who <u>does not **love** does not know God</u>, for God is love. 9 God showed **how much he loved us** by sending his one and only Son into the world so that we might have eternal life through him. 10 **<u>This is real love</u>**—not that we loved God, but that he loved us and sent his Son as a sacrifice to take away our sins. 11 Dear friends, since God loved us that much, **we surely ought to love each other.** 12 No one has ever seen God. But if we love each other, God lives in us, and his love is brought to full expression in us."
1 John 4:7-12

"16 We know how much God **loves** us, and we have put our trust in his love. God is **love**, and all who live in love live in God, and God lives in them. 17 And as we live in God, our love grows more perfect. So we will not be afraid on the day of judgment, but we can face him with confidence because we live like Jesus here in this world. 18 **Such love has no fear**, because perfect love expels all fear. If we are afraid, it is for fear of punishment, and this shows that we have not fully experienced his perfect love. 19 **<u>We love each other because he loved us first.</u>** 20 If someone says, "I love God," but hates a fellow believer, that person is a liar; for if we don't love people we can see, how can we love God, whom we cannot see? 21 And he has given us this command: Those who love God <u>must</u> also love their fellow believers."
1 John 4:16-21

"8 Most important of all, continue to show deep love for each other, for love covers a multitude of sins!"
1 Peter 4:8

"4 Love is patient and kind. Love is not jealous or boastful or proud 5 or rude. It does not demand its own way. It is not irritable, and it keeps no record of being wronged. 6 It does not rejoice about injustice but rejoices whenever the truth wins out. 7 Love never gives up, never loses faith, is always hopeful, and endures through every circumstance." **1 Corinthians 13:4-7**

Prayer

Abba Father, help me to love without walls and conditions. You loved the whole world so much that You gave Your one and only Son knowing that not every heart would love You back. Help me to love those who seem undeserving of my heart. Father sometimes I am scared to love because of the hurt I have endured in the past but I know Your word says that if I do not love then I do not know you for You are LOVE!

May I trust and be rooted in Your love because there is no fear because perfect love expels fear and covers a multitude of sin! Always being patient and kind, never jealous, boastful, proud, or irritable. I will never again hold a record of wrong that has been done because I have surrendered and released my past to you and all future suffering I may endure. May I only rejoice when the truth wins and may I never give up, be forever faithful and hopefully. I will endure in every circumstance because the love of my Father is in me.
In Jesus name. Amen

JESUS, I WILL LOVE UNCONDITIONALLY:

♡

"Love never gives up, never loses faith, is always hopeful, and endures through every circumstance."
1 Corinthians 13:7

ROMANS 8:17

How God Can Turn Your Pain Into Purpose

Study

The Word of God says in Romans 8:17 that if we are to share in His glory, then we will also share in the suffering. Suffering **will** happen- trials and tribulations are a part of the journey of life. We can actually count it ALL joy when these trials come upon us.

"1 Dear brothers and sisters, when troubles of any kind come your way, consider it an opportunity for great joy. 3 For you know that when your faith is tested, your endurance has a chance to grow. 4 So let it grow, for when your endurance is fully developed, you will be perfect and complete, needing nothing." **James 1:2-4**

This is how your pain turns into a true purpose that Abba Father will use to complete you! However you must open your heart to count it joy and allow your faith to be tested so that your endurance can grow and become fully developed. Then when the next trial comes, you will be unmovable, unshakable and rooted in the love of Christ!

"God blesses those who patiently endure testing and temptation. Afterward they will receive the crown of life that God has promised to those who love him."
James 1:12

The Purpose

3 All praise to God, the Father of our Lord Jesus Christ. God is our merciful Father and the source of all comfort. 4 He comforts us in all our troubles so that we can comfort others. When they are troubled, we will be able to give them the same comfort God has given us. 5 For the more we suffer for Christ, the more God will shower us with his comfort through Christ. 6 Even when we are weighed down with troubles, it is for your comfort and salvation! For when we ourselves are comforted, we will certainly comfort you. Then you can patiently endure the same things we suffer. 7 We are confident that as you share in our sufferings, you will also share in the comfort God gives us. **2 Corinthians 1:3-7**

You WILL be comforted by your Heavenly Father. From that point you shall comfort others. The pain and trauma will turn into a purpose- to be a comfort for others! Even Paul said they were crushed and overwhelmed which is how we can feel daily. He said "we expected to die!" There have been days that I am sure we have felt and even **wanted** death to wrap us up HOWEVER- this taught Paul to not rely on himself but to rely solely on the one who raises the dead: GOD!

Will you **surrender** today and rely on God?
Can you **trust and believe** that God can and will turn all that you have endured into a purpose!

God used a donkey to speak.
God sent ravens to feed Elijah.
God caused a sea to split open and gave the Israelites DRY ground to walk on!

So **make a choice** to believe He will do the same for you!
He will turn this pain into a great purpose in You!

You are not alone!

A person standing alone can be attacked and defeated, but two can stand back-to-back and conquer. Three are even better, for a triple-braided cord is not easily broken.
Ecclesiastes 4:12

You do not have to walk through hardships alone. The Lord designed us to be in unity, **together**, and fight our battles in prayer. If you need prayer or desire a deeper relationship with Jesus contact us today.

Contact:

prayer@revivedcommunity.com

revivedcommunity.com

NOTES

NOTES

Made in the USA
Columbia, SC
31 October 2024